FIRST MOTHERS

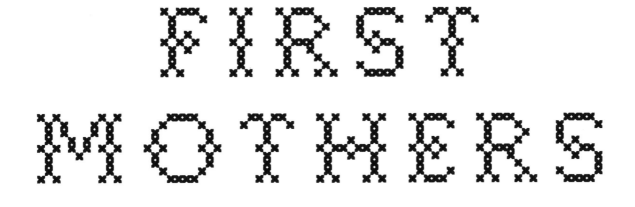

Written by Beverly Gherman

Illustrated by Julie Downing

Clarion Books   Houghton Mifflin Harcourt   Boston New York   2012

Clarion Books
215 Park Avenue South, New York, New York 10003

Text copyright © 2012 by Beverly Gherman
Illustrations copyright © 2012 by Julie Downing

Clarion Books is an imprint of Houghton Mifflin Harcourt Publishing Company.

www.hmhbooks.com

The text in this book was set in Caslon Twelve ITC.
The illustrations were done in watercolor and colored pencil.
Book design by Sharismar Rodriguez

Library of Congress Cataloging-in-Publication Data is available.
LCCN 2012930747

Manufactured in China
LEO 10 9 8 7 6 5 4 3 2 1
4500355406

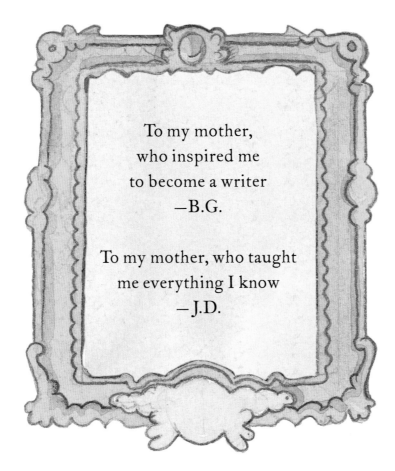

To my mother,
who inspired me
to become a writer
—B.G.

To my mother, who taught
me everything I know
—J.D.

CONTENTS

No. 1: # THE FIRST FIRST MOTHER

Mary Ball Washington

George Washington's mother had a difficult life. She became an orphan at twelve and a widow at thirty-five. Her losses made her a terrible worrier. She worried that her children would drown or fall from a horse or go hungry.

She worried that George would get ill if he went to boarding school in England or that he would go down with his ship in the King's Navy.

Yet despite her fears for her children, she never seemed pleased with their success. No matter how much George accomplished, Mary never told him she was proud of him. She was happy only when he married a wealthy widow, Martha Custis. Now he wouldn't need his mother's money.

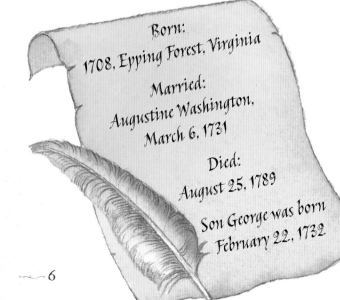

Born:
1708, Epping Forest, Virginia

Married:
Augustine Washington,
March 6, 1731

Died:
August 25, 1789

Son George was born
February 22, 1732

George's friends respected him, even if his mother did not. He was honest, handsome, and a great military leader. He was elected president of the new country. Mary was not impressed.

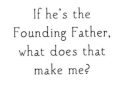

If he's the Founding Father, what does that make me?

AMERICA'S FOUNDING FATHER, *George Washington*, LEADS PATRIOTS TO VICTORY.

THE DETERMINED MOTHER

Susanna Boylston Adams

John Adams's mother was strong-willed. She grew up in a hilltop mansion overlooking Boston, Massachusetts. Many young men climbed the hill asking for her hand, but she did not like any of them.

Marry the one with money!

Born:
March 5, 1708,
Brookline, Massachusetts
Married:
Deacon John Adams,
October 30, 1734
Died:
April 21, 1797
Son John was born
October 19, 1735

Then she met Deacon John Adams. He was perfect! Most of the year, he farmed and made enough money to support a family. In the winter he made fine shoes.

He also found time to be a leader in his church and the community. Susanna could not read or write, but she was determined that her sons would learn to do both.

Deacon John agreed. There was no question that John had to do well because he was to go to Harvard.

Susanna had a terrible temper. She threw a fit over the smallest thing. But she tried to teach her oldest son, John, to control his own temper.

Fortunately Susanna lived just long enough to see John become the second president of the United States. She died six weeks later.

No. 3: THE BUSY MOTHER

Jane Randolph Jefferson

Thomas Jefferson's mother was born into a wealthy Virginia family and grew up on a large plantation. She fell in love with Colonel Peter Jefferson. He didn't have much money, but Jane knew he would be a good husband because he was not afraid to work hard.

Their first home was small, and Jane was busy all the time. She gave birth to nine children—six daughters and three sons. She grew vegetables, planted flowers, and took care of her family, plus her cousin's three children. She taught the girls to card, spin, and wind yarn. She expected her sons to help her with the heavy work of the crops and gardens.

Where's the rest of the house?

Peter died early, and Jane was left a widow at thirty-seven. Even though she needed Thomas's help at home, Jane sent him away to get an education. At sixteen he moved to Williamsburg to attend the College of William and Mary, the second oldest college in the country. She still expected him to come home on weekends to help her.

My son *George* never came home on weekends!

It doesn't seem that Thomas showed his mother any affection or gratitude. When Jane died suddenly of a stroke, Thomas only noted her death in his journal, attended her funeral, and then rushed back to the Continental Congress. He did suffer a severe migraine headache, however, which may have been the way Thomas dealt with his grief.

Born:
February 20, 1720,
Shadwell, London
Married:
Peter Jefferson,
October 3, 1739
Died:
March 31, 1776
Son Thomas was born
April 13, 1743

No. 4: THE AFFECTIONATE MOTHER

Eleanor Rose Conway Madison

James Madison's mother lived a long life and stayed close to her children, though only seven of twelve lived to adulthood. James was especially close to his mother. He called her Nelly. She called him Jemmy.

Born: January 9, 1731,
Port Conway, Virginia

Married: James Monroe,
September 15, 1749

Died: February 11, 1829

Son James was born
March 16, 1751

While Jemmy attended the College of New Jersey, later called Princeton, Nelly stitched shirts for him and made him fresh tubs of butter from their cows.

Nelly treated her servants with kindness and encouraged her children and the servants' children to play with one another.

She told her friends that she had been a "blest woman" all her life.

THE UNKNOWN MOTHER

Elizabeth Jones Monroe

James Monroe's mother came to her marriage with money and property but without good records. It is believed that she was born sometime in 1730, but no one wrote down either the date of her birth or the date of her death. She and her husband had five children and made sure all of them were well educated. It's believed that many evenings by candlelight, Elizabeth read James classical literature.

James was sixteen when his father died. He went on to get a good education at the College of William and Mary, and his uncle, Judge Joseph Jones, made certain that James received the estate his father left him. The money allowed him to become a gentleman.

A GOOD WIFE AND PARENT LIVES HERE.

I don't mind that no one knows anything about me. My son was only the fifth president. I'm just his mother. I'm fine . . . really.

BORN: 1730, KING GEORGE COUNTY, VIRGINIA
MARRIED: SPENCE MONROE, 1752
DIED: 1774
SON JAMES WAS BORN APRIL 28, 1758

No. 6: # THE MODERN MOTHER

Abigail Smith Adams

John Quincy Adams's mother became famous for her letters and ideas. Her father, a minister, believed that his daughters should learn to read and think, even though most young women in the 1750s were not educated at all. In later years she resented the fact that she had never attended school. But despite her lack of formal education, Abigail had bold and modern ideas.

Abigail was only fifteen when she met John Adams. At first she thought he talked too much and acted like a know-it-all.

But by the time she was eighteen she appreciated his intelligence and the books he brought her to read, as well as his sense of humor. They married in 1764 and had four children.

Her husband was elected to the Continental Congress, which met in Philadelphia to form an independent country. Abigail stayed behind in Braintree, Massachusetts. By day, she took care of the farm and the children. At night she wrote John long letters by candlelight. She told him about the family, the farm, what the British troops were doing nearby, and how many British ships could be seen in Boston Harbor.

BORN:
NOVEMBER 22, 1744,
WEYMOUTH, MASSACHUSETTS

MARRIED:
JOHN ADAMS,
OCTOBER 25, 1764

DIED:
OCTOBER 28, 1818

SON JOHN QUINCY WAS BORN
JULY 11, 1767

In one letter, she reminded John that women deserved equal rights. "Remember the Ladies," she wrote. "Do not put such unlimited power into the hands of the Husbands." No matter how important John and John Quincy became, she never hesitated to tell them what to do. She urged them to work to end slavery and told them that "the fortunate must help those who are less fortunate." She and John both believed in putting public service ahead of their personal happiness. She was the first woman to be both the wife and the mother of a president.

THE BRAVE MOTHER

Elizabeth Hutchinson Jackson (Betty)

Andrew Jackson's mother came to America hoping to improve her life. Betty and her husband were linen weavers from Ireland. Unfortunately her husband died while Betty was pregnant with her third son. She named him Andrew after the father he never knew.

Betty expected Andrew to become a minister, but he was more interested in running and riding.

Born: 1737,
Carrickfergus, Ireland

Married:
Andrew Jackson, 1761

Died: November 2, 1781

Son Andrew was born
March 15, 1767

All three of Betty's sons fought against the British during the Revolutionary War. Her oldest was killed in battle. Her two younger sons, Robert, fifteen, and Andrew, just thirteen, joined the patriot militia, but were captured by the British during a raid. The officer in charge demanded that the boys clean his muddy boots, but when they refused, the officer raised his sword and slashed both boys: Andrew on his face, Robert on his body.

When Betty learned that her boys had been captured and taken to a prison camp, she found a patriot officer who agreed to release thirteen British prisoners in exchange for her sons. Robert died soon after they returned home. By now, Betty had lost a husband and two sons. She was not about to lose her youngest, so she spent eight months nursing him back to health. After Andrew was well, Betty left to care for other prisoners. She caught cholera from one of the men and died.

In later life, Andrew would tell people his mother was "as gentle as a dove and as brave as a lioness." She had advised Andrew, "Never tell a lie, nor take what is not your own, nor sue for slander. . . . Settle them cases yourself."

My son was the first president born as a U.S. citizen.

My son was the 9th president and my grandson was the 23rd.

No. 8: THE WORKING MOTHER
Maria Van Buren

Born: February 27, 1747, Claverack, a Dutch village near Kinderhook, New York
Married: Abraham Van Buren, 1776 ❧ Died: February 16, 1817
Son Martin was born December 5, 1782

Martin Van Buren's mother was a widow with three children when she married tavern owner Abraham Van Buren. Although her husband was good-natured, he was a terrible businessman, so it was up to Maria to stretch the tiny amount left to feed their family.

She worked hard in the tavern and raised nine children in two small rooms above the bar. There was no money for college, but she convinced her husband to let Martin stay in school until he was fifteen. Then Maria found her son a job in a law firm so he wouldn't have to work in the tavern. Maria taught her son that he could succeed if he planned carefully and worked harder than other people.

No. 9: THE BEAUTIFUL MOTHER
Elizabeth Bassett Harrison

Born: December 13, 1730, New Kent County, Virginia
Married: Benjamin Harrison, 1748 ❧ Died: 1792
Son William was born February 9, 1773

William Henry Harrison's mother was born into one of the richest families in Virginia. Famous as a local beauty, Elizabeth was eighteen when she married, but her husband, Benjamin, a politician, was away from home most of the time. It was up to Elizabeth to raise their seven children.

As a young wife, she needed help with the cooking and cleaning, because the plantation they lived on was the size of a small town. During the Revolution, the family was forced to leave their home and escape from the oncoming troops.

Though they survived this ordeal, sadly Elizabeth didn't live long enough to see her son become president.

Your son William was only president for a month. Mine became vice president *and* president.

I prayed my son would become a minister, but president will do.

No. 10: THE DREAMER MOTHER
Mary Armistead Tyler

Born: 1761, York County, Virginia
Married: John Tyler, 1776 ❧ Died: April 5, 1797
Son John was born March 29, 1790

No. 11: THE RELIGIOUS MOTHER
Jane Knox Polk

Born: November 15, 1776, Iredell County, North Carolina
Married: Samuel Polk, December 25, 1794 ❧ Died: January 11, 1852
Son James was born November 2, 1795

John Tyler's mother was shy, while her husband, who was much older, talked enough for the two of them. Mary came from a wealthy family and was only sixteen when she married. She and her husband had eight children; John was their sixth.

One evening while Mary held baby John on her lap, he reached up to the moon. Mary said he was reaching so high, she thought it meant he would someday become president. Unfortunately, like many colonial mothers, she died young. She was only thirty-six, and her son was just seven. She never knew that her dreams for her son came true.

James Polk's mother was serious, devout, and believed time spent on anything other than Bible study was a waste. James was the first of ten children.

Meanwhile, the new country was expanding and the Polks wanted a better life. They packed their wagon and traveled 500 miles west from North Carolina to Tennessee. James grew up listening to his parents debate the future of the new country. They believed that one day the frontier would stretch all the way to the Pacific Ocean.

James was as serious and hardworking as his mother. During his campaign, he promised to expand the country, and while president he doubled the size of the United States.

No. 12: THE PIONEER MOTHER
Sarah Dabney Taylor

Born: December 14, 1760, west of Fredericksburg, Virginia
Married: Richard Taylor, August 20, 1779 ✣ Died: December 13, 1822
Son Zachary was born November 24, 1784

Zachary Taylor's mother was used to a genteel life on one of the biggest plantations in Virginia. But when her husband moved the family to the wilds of Kentucky, Sarah learned to be a strong pioneer woman. Instead of fancy food and grand balls, she learned to live with poisonous snakes and the constant fear of encounters with Indians.

There were no nearby schools, so Sarah was her children's only teacher. If it hadn't been for his mother, Zachary Taylor would not have learned to read or write.

No. 13: THE STRUGGLING MOTHER
Phoebe Millard Fillmore

Born: August 12, 1781, Pittsfield, Massachusetts
Married: Nathaniel Fillmore, 1796 ✣ Died: May 2, 1831
Son Millard was born January 7, 1800

Millard Fillmore's mother grew up in a middle class family. But Phoebe said goodbye to comfort when her husband, Nathaniel, bought land at a bargain price in New York State, where the soil was so rocky that nothing grew. As a result Phoebe struggled to feed her nine children.

Phoebe taught her children to read using the only books she brought from home—the almanac, her Bible, and a hymn book. Millard never saw a map of the United States until he was twenty. When he lived in the White House, Fillmore established the first library.

No. 14: THE FLAMBOYANT MOTHER
Anna Kendrick Pierce

Born: October 30, 1768, Hillsborough, New Hampshire
Married: Benjamin Pierce, February 1, 1790 ❧ Died: December 7, 1838
Son Franklin was born November 23, 1804

Franklin Pierce's mother loved to have fun. Anna and her husband were some of the first settlers in New Hampshire. Her Puritan neighbors wore dark colors and did not believe in dancing or drinking. Anna loved to shock them by wearing bright colors and skirts short enough to show her ankles. People talked about her all the time. Sometimes the gossip bothered Anna, but not enough to change. Franklin told people he inherited his lively personality from his mother.

No. 15: THE POETIC MOTHER
Elizabeth Speer Buchanan

Born: March 17, 1767, Lancaster County, Pennsylvania
Married: James Buchanan, 1788 ❧ Died: May 14, 1833
Son James was born April 23, 1791

James Buchanan's mother was curious about everything. Eliza never went to school but taught herself to read and memorized pages of poems, which she recited to her eleven children. When James was born, the family was living at a trading post in rural Pennsylvania, and Eliza was his first teacher. James said his mother argued "about everything," because she wanted to teach him to defend his ideas. Later, when he became a politician, he was known as a gifted debater.

No. 16: THE STRONG MOTHER
Nancy Hanks Lincoln

Abraham Lincoln's mother was good at many things. Nancy was a fine seamstress and had a beautiful singing voice. She read the Bible to the children, taught them to read, and treated them with sweetness.

Abe's father did not believe in education, but his mother insisted that Abe and his sister go to school. They walked nine miles each way to get there.

Nancy was strong and had been a wrestler in her early life. She outwrestled many of the men in her town.

Born: February 5, 1784, Pipers Gap, Virginia
Married: Thomas Lincoln, June 12, 1806
Died: October 5, 1818
Son Abraham was born February 12, 1809

Grateful for his education, Abraham carried a book with him wherever he went and always said, "God bless my mother. All I am or ever hope to be, I owe to her." She died when he was nine years old.

THE STEPMOTHER

Sarah Bush Johnston Lincoln

Abraham was ten when his father remarried. His stepmother, Sarah, brought wonderful treasures with her: pillows, blankets, and glassware. Best of all, she brought books. As soon as Abe saw her, he ran and hugged her. She quickly organized their log cabin, fixed their meals, and brought the family love and affection.

Sarah had a wonderful sense of humor, and she teased Abe that he had grown so tall, his head was going to dirty her whitewashed ceilings. One day Abe played a joke on her. He held a boy up and had him "walk" across the ceiling. When Sarah saw the footprints, she laughed for an hour.

Abraham was lucky to have both a mother and a stepmother who loved him and encouraged him.

Although Sarah normally didn't have premonitions, just before his inauguration, she warned Abe to be careful. She was worried that something bad was going to happen.

Born: December 13, 1788, Elizabethtown, Kentucky
Married: Thomas Lincoln, December 2, 1819
Died: April 12, 1869

No. 17: THE RESOURCEFUL MOTHER
Mary McDonough Johnson (Polly)

Andrew Johnson's mother wanted to give her son a better life. Polly was a maid at the local inn. She washed and mended clothes for neighbors in her spare time, and even took up spinning and weaving to make extra money. Polly's husband died when Andrew was only three. As a poor widow, she did what many women had to do: she remarried. Unfortunately her new husband was lazy and mean, and now she had to support him as well.

Polly wanted her sons to get an education but could not afford to give it to them. Andrew never went to a single day of school in his whole life! Instead she apprenticed him to a tailor. Eventually he opened his own successful tailor's shop and got involved in local politics.

Like his mother, Johnson was resourceful and hardworking. He proved that you did not need a family name or family money to become president.

BORN: JULY 17, 1783, UNKNOWN
MARRIED: JACOB JOHNSON,
SEPTEMBER 9, 1801
DIED: FEBRUARY 13, 1856
SON ANDREW WAS BORN
DECEMBER 29, 1808

No. 18: THE QUIET MOTHER
Hannah Simpson Grant

Ulysses S. Grant's mother was shy and quiet. Hannah seldom spoke, even to her children. The neighbors thought she was a bad parent because she didn't shower any of her six children with hugs. Instead, she gave them all great freedom to explore. When Ulysses was a young toddler she let him crawl around the family stables, and that also caused the neighbors to wonder about her child-rearing habits.

Hannah did not believe in bragging about her children. She chose to remain silent even when Ulysses attended West Point or became general of the Union army.

After Ulysses became president, his father, Jesse, often visited him in the White House and chatted with the reporters, but Hannah was too shy to go and did not even attend his presidential inauguration.

It's not right to brag, but Ulysses was a good boy.

BORN: NOVEMBER 23, 1798,
BERKS COUNTY, PENNSYLVANIA
MARRIED: JESSE GRANT,
JUNE 24, 1821
DIED: MAY 11, 1883
SON ULYSSES WAS BORN
APRIL 27, 1822

THE PROTECTIVE MOTHER

Sophia Birchard Hayes

Born: April 15, 1792, Wilmington, Vermont ❧ Married: Rutherford Hayes, September 13, 1813
Died: October 30, 1866 ❧ Son Rutherford was born October 4, 1822

Rutherford Hayes's mother knew her job was to keep her son Ruddy alive and healthy. Everyone else in Sophia's life had died, including her husband and two of her children. In those years, there were no vaccines or medicines to prevent the spread of diseases. All the losses in her own life made Sophia fearful for her two remaining children. She decided to educate Ruddy and his sister at home, rarely letting them out of her sight.

She finally allowed Ruddy to get a public school education at fourteen. He then became interested in the law and politics, and in becoming a soldier— exactly what Sophia had worried about.

When Ruddy fought in the Civil War, Sophia spent time on her knees praying for his safety. He was spared and returned to serve as a congressman, but she did not live to see him elected president.

Shouldn't your son help?

No. 20: THE INDUSTRIOUS MOTHER

Elizabeth Ballou Garfield

Born: September 21, 1801, Richmond, New Hampshire ✣ Married: Abram Garfield, February 3, 1820
Died: January 21, 1888 ✣ Son James was born November 19, 1831

James Garfield's mother endured more heartache than most people.
As a young bride she survived malaria and a fire that burned down her first
home. Just two years after the birth of their youngest son, James, Eliza's
husband died and left her with four children. Eliza took over the farm,
splitting logs, building fences, and harvesting wheat. She and her daughters
carded wool from their sheep. She wove all their clothing and sold extra
garments to make money.

Eliza had a beautiful singing voice and knew so many hymns and ballads
that she could sing for forty-eight hours without repeating a song. No matter
how hard life became, Eliza faced the future cheerfully.

Shortly after he became president, James Garfield was assassinated by an
angry voter. Sadly, Eliza watched her son suffer for a month before he died.
She lived six years after his death.

No. 21: THE WRITER MOTHER
Malvina Stone Arthur

Chester Arthur's mother, Malvina, was eighteen when she fell in love with William Arthur, a handsome Irish schoolteacher who was studying law. But after a religious revival meeting, Malvina's husband was deeply moved and decided he was destined to preach rather than become a lawyer.

Born:
April 29, 1802,
Berkshire Township, Vermont

Married:
William Arthur,
April 12, 1821

Died: January 16, 1869
Son Chester was born
October 5, 1829

The family moved across the Vermont countryside, where William delivered sermons and Malvina delivered babies. The couple had nine children; Chester was their fifth and first son.

Malvina was religious and taught all her children to pray and stay away from alcohol and gambling. She also taught her children that slavery was wrong and that they should respect people, no matter what color their skin.

Before becoming president, Chester was a New York lawyer. He won an important case that ended racial segregation on streetcars. When the public worried that Chester had not been born in the United States and could not become president, Malvina's letters proved that he was a citizen.

THE SACRIFICING MOTHER

Ann Neal Cleveland

Born: February 4, 1806, Baltimore, Maryland ⚭ Married: Richard Cleveland, September 10, 1829
Died: July 19, 1882 ⚭ Son Grover was born March 18, 1837

Grover Cleveland's mother was the daughter of a prosperous Baltimore publisher and was used to expensive things. Ann fell in love and married a serious young minister because he seemed so different from the young men she met. The newlyweds moved to Connecticut for his first job. She arrived with trunks full of silk dresses and colorful jewelry. As soon as she unpacked, the women in her new parish let her know that no decent clergyman's wife ever wore such expensive things.

Ann listened and sent everything back to Baltimore. Instead of dinner parties and dances, Ann devoted herself to raising nine children on a minister's small salary. She was a strict parent and did not believe in useless activities such as sports or games. Instead she insisted her children memorize huge chunks of the Bible.

When he became president, Grover said his mother's prayers brought him all his success.

No. 23: THE CAUTIOUS MOTHER

Elizabeth Irwin Harrison

Born: July 18, 1810, Mercersburg, Pennsylvania ⚭ Married: John Harrison, August 12, 1831
Died: August 15, 1850 ⚭ Son Benjamin was born August 20, 1833

Benjamin Harrison's mother spent long hours each day praying for her ten children and two stepchildren. When Benjamin went to college, she cautioned him not to sin or stray from the paths of duty. She even warned him to watch his diet and stay away from cucumbers. She thought they were very bad for you.

Elizabeth died when Benjamin was only seventeen. He did not listen to her warnings about politics, but he did inherit her formal personality. Some people called him the "human iceberg."

No. 25: THE PRACTICAL MOTHER

Nancy Allison McKinley

Born: April 22, 1809, Ohio Frontier ❧ Married: William McKinley, January 6, 1829
Died: December 12, 1897 ❧ Son William was born January 29, 1843

William McKinley's mother did not raise her son to be president. Nancy told
people she just wanted her son to be a good man. She raised nine children
to be as hardworking and thrifty as she was. When Nancy attended
her son's presidential inauguration, she carried a bouquet of lovely roses.
She had arrived by train and did not see the sense in buying flowers
for the event, so she simply used the flowers from the train's dining car.

No. 26: THE SOUTHERN MOTHER
Martha Bulloch Roosevelt (Mittie)

President Theodore Roosevelt's mother was tiny
and beautiful with a strong mind of her own.

Mittie was fifteen when she first met his
father, also named Theodore, who was already
twenty. She thought he was boring. He kept
spouting the Latin names of plants he saw.
She wanted him to be like her brothers,
who danced and joked and played
musical instruments. Though she was
born in Connecticut, Mittie grew up
in Savannah, Georgia, and was a true
southern belle.

A perfect
example
of *Rosa
berberifolia.*

She and Theodore met again two years later. By then she found him more spirited and accepted his invitation to visit his family in New York City. Once she returned home, they sent each other frequent love letters. She called him "Dearest Thee."

After they married, they had four children. As the children grew up, they tried to understand their parents' confusing Civil War talk. They knew Mittie's brothers were fighting for the South and she often sent them care packages. But their father supported the Union and disapproved of slavery.

In February 1884, Mittie came down with typhoid fever. At the same time, Theodore Jr.'s wife, Alice, gave birth to a daughter. But before the family could celebrate, Alice fell ill with kidney disease and Mittie grew weaker and weaker. They both died on February fourteenth. Mittie died in the morning. Alice died in the afternoon. The future president never got over his loss.

Born: July 8, 1835,
Hartford, Connecticut
Married: Theodore Roosevelt Sr.,
December 22, 1853
Died: February 14, 1884
Son Theodore Jr. was born
October 27, 1858

No. 27: THE STYLISH MOTHER

Louisa Torrey Taft

Born: September 11, 1827, Millbury, Massachusetts ❧ Married: Alphonso Taft, December 26, 1853
Died: December 8, 1907 ❧ Son William Howard was born September 15, 1857

William Taft's mother was an old maid at twenty-six. She loved to travel and shop and vowed never to marry. She especially liked buying the latest fashions, but when she could not afford a new French hat, she realized she would either have to cut back on her luxuries or find a husband to pay for them.

When Louisa met Alphonso Taft, she thought he was comical—so tall and so heavy. But as she got to know him better, she stopped noticing how large he was. She enjoyed talking to him about law, politics, and women's rights.

They married and had five children; four lived to adulthood. Louisa made sure she always wore the latest fashions.

My son proclaimed May 9, 1914, as the first Mother's Day in honor of all mothers, but especially me.

No. 28: THE ADORING MOTHER

Jesse Woodrow Wilson

Born: December 20, 1830, Carlisle, England
Married: Joseph Wilson, June 7, 1849 ♣ Died: April 15, 1888
Son Thomas Woodrow was born December 28, 1856

Woodrow Wilson's mother thought her son was perfect. Jesse adored all four of her children, but especially her oldest son, Thomas Woodrow. From the beginning, Jesse bragged about what "a fine healthy fellow" he was. When he had difficulty reading because he saw words backwards, Jesse read aloud to him. Thomas didn't learn to read on his own until he was nine. Jesse's husband, a southern minister, constantly told his son to strive to be the best. Jesse, on the other hand, already thought her "darling boy" was the best. In fact, she told him not to be too ambitious, for fear it might cause him worry or unhappiness.

No. 29: THE MIDWIFE MOTHER

Phoebe Dickerson Harding

Born: December 21, 1843, Blooming Grove, Ohio
Married: Tyron Harding, May 7, 1864 ♣ Died: May 20, 1910
Son Warren was born November 2, 1865

Warren Harding's mother secretly eloped when she was twenty. Her parents were surprised, but Phoebe was used to getting what she wanted. When she decided it was time for her first son, Warren, to learn to read, she sat him on her knee and read Bible stories aloud until he learned. When her husband did not make enough money to support their eight children, Phoebe made money delivering babies and eventually became a doctor. Warren might have been a better president if he had inherited his mother's determination. Some historians think he was one of our worst presidents because he did not stand up for his ideas.

I taught my son to be careful with money. He was the only president who saved any of his salary.

No. 30: THE INVALID MOTHER

Victoria Moor Coolidge

Born: March 14, 1846, Pinney Hollow, Vermont ⚭ Married: John Coolidge, May 6, 1868
Died: March 14, 1885 ⚭ Son, Calvin, was born July 4, 1872

Calvin Coolidge's mother was named for European royalty, but there was nothing regal in her upbringing. Victoria grew up on a farm in rural Vermont, where she met her husband, John. They had two children, Calvin and Abigail. Farm life was constant work, but Victoria taught her children to notice the sunsets and the beauty of the night sky. Victoria suffered from tuberculosis and had to spend most of her time resting quietly, so when Calvin was young she taught him to sew. Together they made a quilt.

Victoria died when Calvin was only twelve. He missed her so much that he carried her picture with him for his entire life.

My son, Herbert, began construction on the San Francisco Bay Bridge.

No. 31: THE IDEALISTIC MOTHER

Hulda Minthorn Hoover

Born: May 4, 1848, Ontario, Canada ❧ Married: Jesse Hoover, 1870
Died: February 24, 1883 ❧ Son Herbert was born August 10, 1874

Herbert Hoover's mother seemed quiet and gentle, but Hulda was not afraid to tell people what she thought. She introduced her son to politics when he was only six. Women were not allowed to vote, so Hulda and Herbert stood outside crowded polling places and persuaded men to vote for Prohibition, a law that made alcohol illegal. She used any opportunity to preach her values and became an outspoken minister. One stormy night, after preaching to a congregation, Hulda walked home in the rain. A few days later she caught pneumonia and died. Although she died when Herbert was only eight, Hulda gave her son the foundation for his interest in politics.

THE BOSSY MOTHER

Sara Delano Roosevelt

Franklin Roosevelt's mother loved to tell people what to do, especially her son, Franklin. Sara considered herself an expert on marriage, child rearing, politics, and current affairs. Even though she had only one child, she wrote articles for new mothers about raising their infants.

At fourteen, Franklin went to Groton Boarding School. Sara and his father, James, were traveling in Europe when they learned Franklin was ill with scarlet fever. Sara rushed back and insisted on caring for her son, but the doctors said she could not see him because he was quarantined in the infirmary. Sara found a way to visit him anyway!

Born:
September 21, 1854,
Newburgh, New York

Married:
James Roosevelt,
October 7, 1880

Died:
September 7, 1941

Son, Franklin, was
born January 30,
1882

Franklin married his cousin Eleanor on March 17, 1905. One summer when Franklin, Eleanor, and their children were vacationing on Campobello Island, off the coast of Maine, Franklin came down with polio. At thirty-nine, his legs were paralyzed and he was unable to walk. Even though he was in a wheelchair, Franklin became president of the United States in 1932. But it was Sara's picture that appeared on the cover of *Time* magazine.

On November 8, 1932, Sara was the first mother to vote for her son for president.

Throughout his presidency, Sara was still
advising Franklin on how to handle difficult
situations. He listened and then followed
his own ideas. In the summer of 1941,
Franklin went to see Sara, who was ailing.
He told her about his earlier visit with the
English prime minister, Winston Churchill,
who was fighting Nazi Germany and
wanted help from the United States.
Sara scolded Franklin for not bringing
Churchill to see her. She would have told
Churchill how to fight the war.

Sara died the next day, two weeks before
her eighty-seventh birthday.

No. 33: THE LIVELY MOTHER
Martha Young Truman (Mattie)

Harry Truman's mother loved to ride a horse and shoot a rifle. She learned to cook and sew like most young women of her generation, but really she wanted to be outside riding across her family's six-hundred-acre farm.

When she became a mother, Mattie let her own children have lots of freedom to explore. She did not worry about them. She knew they would come home when they were hungry. Harry and his two siblings had chores, but once the work was done, Mattie sat at the piano and played their favorite tunes. She took her children on picnics and to church socials. They had a very happy childhood.

One July fourth, Mattie noticed Harry was ignoring the brilliant fireworks. The very next day she rushed Harry to an eye specialist in Kansas City. The doctor made Harry thick glasses for his weak eyes. Soon he was reading books, noticing the stars in the sky, and watching the horses in the pasture.

Hold on, Harry!

Where's the fire?

Mattie was ninety-four when she flew for the first time to visit Harry at the White House. When she saw the large crowd waiting to meet her, she said, "Oh, fiddlesticks." She would have stayed home if she had known there would be such a fuss.

WESTERN UNION

Born: November 25, 1852, Jackson County, Missouri

Married: John Truman, December 28, 1881

Died: July 26, 1947

Son Harry was born May 8, 1884

No. 34: THE PACIFIST MOTHER
Ida Stover Eisenhower

Dwight Eisenhower's mother did not believe in war. Ida grew up during the Civil War, and her father and seven brothers refused to fight for either side. Their religion taught them that war was wrong, no matter what the circumstances. Ida remained a pacifist throughout her life.

Ida's mother and father died when she was young. She and her brothers were sent to live with their strict grandparents. Ida was punished if she burned the biscuits or left dust on the picture frames. Her grandparents encouraged her to read, but only from the Bible. Ida longed to escape and dreamed of going to college. When she turned twenty-one, she took some of the money her father had left her and paid her own tuition.

I marched against war, but my son was a five-star general. I chose my way; Ike should follow his own dreams.

Ida met David Eisenhower at college. They fell in love, married, and ended up in Abilene, Kansas, with six sons and a house with no plumbing.

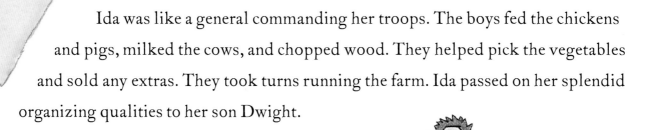

Next!

Ida was like a general commanding her troops. The boys fed the chickens and pigs, milked the cows, and chopped wood. They helped pick the vegetables and sold any extras. They took turns running the farm. Ida passed on her splendid organizing qualities to her son Dwight.

She found joy in her life no matter how hard she worked. Her sons said, "She smiled as easily as she breathed."

Ida was proud of all her sons, not just Dwight. Each of them had a successful life.

Born: May 1, 1862,
Mount Sidney, Virginia
Married: David Eisenhower,
September 23, 1885
Died: September 11, 1946
Son Dwight was born
October 14, 1890

No. 35: THE SAVVY MOTHER
Rose Fitzgerald Kennedy

John Kennedy's mother raised one president, three senators, and two presidential candidates. Rose grew up with politics. Her father, Honey Fitz, was the mayor of Boston, and as a teenager Rose often went with him to political events and parties.

She married Joe Kennedy, who became a bank president and went on to make a fortune. He was a good father, but not such a reliable husband. He had affairs with many glamorous women. So Rose decided that being a mother was her most important job. She raised nine children. She expected them to do well in school, help out at home, and discuss politics at the dinner table.

The Kennedys were very wealthy, but Rose made the children work hard for their allowance. They were paid ten cents a week. When John wanted an increase to forty cents, he had to write his mother a letter. Bobby made extra money selling magazines in his fancy neighborhood, but he decided it would be more efficient if the chauffeur drove him around.

Rose campaigned for John when he ran for Congress in 1946. She dressed differently for each audience, wearing a simple skirt and sweater for working-class people and changing into a suit, jewels, and a fur jacket for fancier groups. She gave teas, and people came in large numbers just to meet her. The opponent said he lost because of those "damn tea parties."

Rose Kennedy's life was one of extremes. She had the greatest joy when she saw her son John inaugurated as president on January 20, 1961.

She experienced tremendous grief when her first son died in World War II; her oldest daughter, Rosemary, was institutionalized; her daughter Kathleen was killed in an accident; John was assassinated; and Bobby was shot and killed during his campaign for president.

RKF

Born: July 22, 1890, Boston, Massachusetts

Married: Joseph Kennedy, October 7, 1914

Died: January 22, 1995

Son John Fitzgerald was born May 29, 1917

No. 36: THE STRIVING MOTHER
Rebekah Baines Johnson

Lyndon Johnson's mother had big plans for her son. Rebekah was determined that he would be someone special, maybe even president of the United States.

Rebekah taught her son the alphabet at two, made him recite poetry at three, and enrolled him in kindergarten at four. When he was older, she insisted he play the violin and take dancing lessons. Finally Lyndon rebelled. To punish him, Rebekah ignored him for weeks at a time.

Born:
June 26, 1881,
McKinney, Texas
Married:
Samuel Johnson Jr.,
August 20, 1907
Died:
September 12, 1958
Son Lyndon was born
August 27, 1908

Rebekah had high standards for herself as well. She had gone to college and dreamed of becoming a writer. After graduating, Rebekah wrote articles for a local paper. One day she interviewed Sam Johnson, a Texas legislator and son of one of the state's biggest cattle ranchers. She was fascinated with Sam's straight talk. They married and moved to his farm in the Texas hill country. Rebekah was disappointed. There was no grand ranch house, only a run-down cabin with a dirt floor.

Unfortunately Sam and Rebekah were very different people. Sam liked drinking with his friends and fighting against groups like the Ku Klux Klan, who were trying to harm local citizens. Rebekah liked art and music. She coached the school debate team and started poetry readings. She also wrote for the weekly newspaper, which her husband bought for her. Most people thought women should not be in journalism, so Rebekah used her initials, *RBJ*, when she wrote articles.

Even after Lyndon became a politician and won a seat in Congress, Rebekah still expected him to do his best. She edited his speeches and reminded him to stand up straight.

Johnson City Gazette

JOHNSON ELECTED

LYNDON JOHNSON WINS ELECTION

by RBJ

—Mother tells son to "stand up straight"
—Johnson wins congressional seat

No. 37: ## THE BAKING MOTHER

Hannah Milhous Nixon

Born: March 7, 1885, Jennings County, Indiana ✤ Married: Frank Nixon, June 25, 1908
Died: September 30, 1967 ✤ Son Richard was born January 9, 1913

Richard Nixon's mother baked fifty pies a day. Each morning at four a.m.
Hannah tied on her apron, lit the oven, and made dozens of pies. She sold her
homemade desserts at the family's small gas station, and the neighbors bought
every single one. Hannah was the family breadwinner, because her husband
had a hard time making a living. The family was so poor that the boys passed
along their old shoes to the next younger brother.

Somehow Hannah saved as many pennies as she could to make certain her
sons could go to college.

Hannah died the year before her son was inaugurated president.

No. 38: # THE OPTIMISTIC MOTHER

Dorothy Gardner Ford

Born: February 28, 1892, Harvard, Illinois ✣ Married: Leslie Lynch King, September 7, 1912 ✣ Divorced: 1915
Married: Gerald R. Ford, February 1, 1917 ✣ Died: September 17, 1967 ✣ Son Gerald was born July 14, 1913

Gerald Ford's mother tried to be positive no matter what was happening. Twenty days after her wedding, Dorothy discovered that her new husband was abusive. In 1913 most young women stayed in bad marriages, but after their son, Leslie, was born, she was afraid her husband would hurt their child. It took courage, but one night she sneaked out of the house with her baby and never went back.

Two years later she met and married Gerald Ford. He adopted Dorothy's son Leslie, and the boy became Gerald Ford Jr. They had three more sons.

Dorothy encouraged Gerald and his brothers not to wring their hands when they lost a game or failed a test and to live by the Ford family motto: "Work hard, tell the truth, and don't be late for dinner."

Dorothy kept busy helping others. She sat in the same church pew for years. One Sunday she died there, waiting for the service to begin.

THE INDEPENDENT MOTHER

Lillian Gordy Carter (Bessie)

Jimmy Carter's mother grew up when most women did not have careers, but Lillian had made up her mind to become a nurse. Her parents thought nurses did all the dirty work and no one appreciated them, but Lillian did not listen. She moved to Plains, Georgia, and studied nursing at a local hospital.

While she was a student, she met James Earl Carter. She did not like his looks, but he kept sending notes and flowers and asking her to marry him, so she finally said yes. They had a happy marriage, dancing, playing poker, and rooting for their favorite baseball team, the Dodgers.

Their oldest son, Jimmy, was born in the hospital where Lillian worked. In the 1920s most women delivered their babies at home, so Lillian liked to brag that he was the first president born in a hospital.

The Carters lived on a big peanut farm outside of Plains. They had no electricity and no indoor plumbing. They used an outhouse. It had two high seats for the parents and two low seats for the children.

Nights and weekends, Lillian worked even harder. The South was still segregated, and many white doctors would not care for African American patients. Lillian delivered babies and took care of her black neighbors. Many could not afford medical care, so she paid for their medical supplies with the money she made from nursing.

After Earl died, Lillian lost interest in the things she enjoyed. She missed her husband. Finally, at sixty-eight, Lillian joined the Peace Corps and went to India. She was horrified by the poverty but felt she was making a difference in people's lives. She stayed two years and came back in time to help Jimmy with his campaign for president.

She often told people, "Don't get stuck in a rocking chair. Always support the issues you care about."

BORN: AUGUST 15, 1889, RICHLAND, GEORGIA

MARRIED: JAMES EARL CARTER, SEPTEMBER 27, 1923

DIED: OCTOBER 30, 1938

SON JIMMY WAS BORN OCTOBER 1, 1924

No. 40: THE DRAMATIC MOTHER
Nelle Clyde Reagan

Ronald Reagan's mother loved to be onstage. Nelle starred in dozens of plays and gave dramatic readings for local ladies' groups. Sometimes Nelle played the banjo while Ron, who was just five, recited poetry.

The theater gave Nelle an escape from her everyday life. She grew up in a strict household and had to leave school at twelve so she could help at home. Life was not easier after she married. Nelle's husband, Jack, drank, and the family moved every time he got a new job. The theater gave her a place to be somebody.

Aside from the theater, her church was the center of Nelle's life. She was a member of the Disciples, a Christian sect. Her religion told her to take care of people less fortunate. She prayed for her neighbors when they were ill and even brought home prisoners who were on parole because she believed that being in a home helped men adjust to life outside prison.

Yet she and her husband struggled to make enough money to keep food on their table. When Jack lost his job selling shoes, Nelle had to sew and do alterations to bring in money. She put cardboard into the soles of her sons' shoes to make them last longer.

In 1918 Nelle became deathly ill with influenza. The epidemic had already killed 500,000 people in the United States. Every night the family prayed at her bedside.

At the time, no one knew about the connection between penicillin and mold, but her doctor told her husband to feed her as much moldy cheese as she could eat. No one knew whether the moldy cheese or the prayers helped, but Nelle survived.

Nelle was very proud of her son when he became a professional actor. She loved to visit the movie set and watch Ron perform. Unfortunately she did not live long enough to see her son become governor of California or president. Like his mother, Ronald Reagan was a natural storyteller, and when he was president, people called him the "Great Communicator."

BORN:
July 24, 1883,
Fulton, Illinois

MARRIED:
Jack Reagan,
November 1904

DIED:
July 25, 1962

Son Ronald was born
February 6, 1911

THE COMPETITIVE MOTHER
Dorothy Walker Bush

George H.W. Bush's mother was a great athlete. Dottie beat almost everybody at golf and tennis. She was a good swimmer and a strong horsewoman. They say that she was nine months pregnant when she joined a softball game, hit a home run, and then was rushed to the hospital to give birth to the first of her five children.

FAX TRANSMISSION

<u>Born</u>: July 1, 1901,
Walker's Point,
York County, Maine

<u>Married</u>: Prescott Bush,
August 6, 1921

<u>Died</u>: November 19, 1992

Son George Herbert Walker
was born June 12, 1924

Born to a well-to-do banking family, Dottie was treated like royalty while growing up. She and her sister, Nancy, attended private schools and were sent to Europe to shop for the latest fashions. When Dottie returned from her travels, she wanted to attend Vassar College, but like many wealthy young women, she was sent to Miss Porter's social training school to learn to be a good wife and mother. She fell in love with Prescott Bush when she was only eighteen. They were married after dating for two years. Dottie continued to educate herself without attending a university.

Dottie taught her own children to think of other people's needs and to know how lucky they were. As competitive as she was on the tennis courts, she wanted them to know that winning was not everything. "La-dee-da!" she would say if she heard them brag. Dottie never allowed them to show off their accomplishments, even when they were adults. Love and discipline were qualities Dottie insisted upon.

When her son was the liaison to China, Dottie went to Beijing. At seventy-three she rode her bicycle to see the Great Hall of the People. Even after her husband died, she was still bicycling around Maine.

THE CONFIDENT MOTHER
Virginia Clinton Kelley

Bill Clinton's mother worked hard and played hard. Virginia was a good student. She gave birth to Bill three months after his father, Bill Blythe, a recent World War II veteran, died in a car accident. When Bill was three, Virginia, a single mother, left him with his grandmother and went to New Orleans to get a degree in nursing anesthesia. She wanted more financial security.

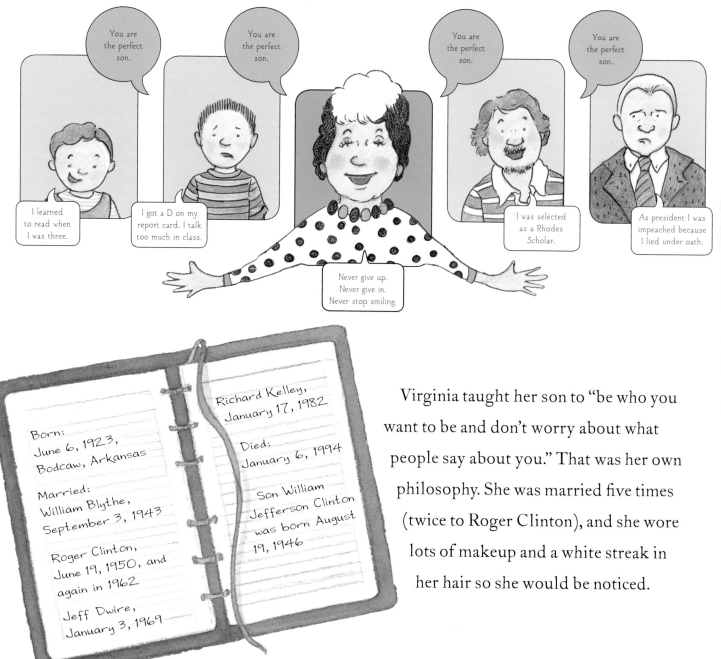

Born:
June 6, 1923,
Bodcaw, Arkansas

Married:
William Blythe,
September 3, 1943

Roger Clinton,
June 19, 1950, and
again in 1962

Jeff Dwire,
January 3, 1969

Richard Kelley,
January 17, 1982

Died:
January 6, 1994

Son William
Jefferson Clinton
was born August
19, 1946

Virginia taught her son to "be who you want to be and don't worry about what people say about you." That was her own philosophy. She was married five times (twice to Roger Clinton), and she wore lots of makeup and a white streak in her hair so she would be noticed.

Even after being diagnosed with cancer, Virginia tried to stay positive and find joy every day. At her funeral, the minister said that Virginia was "like a rubber ball. The harder life put her down, the higher she bounced."

No. 43: THE OUTSPOKEN MOTHER
Barbara Pierce Bush

George W. Bush's mother told people what was on her mind. Sometimes she snapped at reporters or got into trouble for criticizing a political opponent, but voters loved her honesty. She was one of history's most popular first ladies.

Growing up, Barbara believed her sister was her mother's favorite. Martha was pretty, talented, and slim, while Barbara had problems with her weight.

Born: June 8, 1925,
Flushing, New York

Married: George H. W. Bush,
January 6, 1945

Son George Walker was born
July 6, 1946

As an adult she finally stopped worrying about her size. When her husband ran for president in 1988, his advisers thought she should change her style. Barbara agreed to do anything except dye her hair or go on a diet. She told them she was fine just the way she was.

By the time of her husband's election, Barbara had lived in twenty-eight different homes in seventeen cities from Houston to Beijing during her then forty-three years of marriage. She often told people that while her husband was having an exciting time, she was at home with "diapers, runny noses, and earaches."

The Bush family spent summers in Maine. Barbara drove all the way from Texas. She hired two African American women to help with her five children. When they weren't allowed to stay at certain motels because of their skin color, Barbara wouldn't stay either. She told the motel owners she would find a place that would take them all.

Barbara thought her son George was the most like her of all her children. "I've got my father's eyes and my mother's mouth," he said. At school, George became the class clown, and Barbara was often called into the principal's office to talk about her disruptive son. But she always appreciated his sense of humor and was not afraid to give him motherly advice, even when he became president of the United States.

THE ADVENTUROUS MOTHER

Stanley Ann Dunham

Barack Obama's mother was curious about the way people lived. Stanley Ann was not content to read about other cultures; she wanted to travel the world and see them for herself.

Stanley Ann was an only child. Her father had wanted a boy, so he named his daughter Stanley, after himself. He was a furniture salesman, and his job forced the family to move many times. Each time Stanley Ann went to a different school, her new classmates teased her about her name. Finally, in high school, she changed her name to Ann.

Born: November 29, 1942, Wichita, Kansas
Married: Barack Obama, February 2, 1961
Divorced: January 1964
Married: Lolo Soetoro, 1965
Divorced: November 5, 1980
Died: November 7, 1995
Son, Barack, was born August 4, 1961

While attending the University of Hawaii, Ann met a graduate student from Kenya named Barack Obama. Ann's parents did not approve, because Obama was black and Ann was white, but the couple married anyway. Their son, Barack, was born that summer. Ann divorced her husband three years later. After her divorce, Ann became interested in studying how craftspeople make their living. She, her son, and her new husband, Lolo, moved to Indonesia. Ann and Barack were the first foreigners to live in their Jakarta neighborhood. Together they explored the country and learned to speak their new language. Ann worried about her son's education. She woke him at four a.m. every morning and helped him study. She read him speeches by famous Americans like Dr. Martin Luther King. Barack wanted to be a basketball player. His mother told him he'd have to accomplish more than that with his life.

Ann spent thirteen years studying and writing a 1,000-page thesis on metal crafts in Indonesia. She received her Ph.D. and became Dr. Ann Dunham. She also established a program that helped local craftswomen borrow money to start their own businesses.

Ann died of cancer when she was only fifty-two.

BIBLIOGRAPHY

Angelo, Bonnie. *First Mothers: The Women Who Shaped the Presidents.* New York: William Morrow, HarperCollins Publishers Inc., 2000.

Bober, Natalie S. *Thomas Jefferson: Man on a Mountain.* New York: Atheneum, 1988.

Brookhiser, Richard. *America's First Dynasty: The Adamses, 1735–1918.* New York: Free Press, 2002.

Bush, Barbara. *A Memoir.* New York: Scribner, 1994.

Butterfield, L. H., Marc Friedlaender, and Mary-Jo Kline. *The Book of Abigail & John: Selected Letters of the Adams Family, 1762–1784.* Cambridge, Massachusetts: Harvard University Press, 1975.

Carter, Jimmy. *An Hour Before Daylight: Memories of a Rural Boyhood.* New York: Simon & Schuster, 2001.

Gullan, Harold I. *Faith of Our Mothers: The Stories of Presidential Mothers from Mary Washington to Barbara Bush.* Grand Rapids, Michigan: W. B. Eerdmans, 2001.

Lederer, Richard. *Presidential Trivia: The Feats, Fates, Families, Foibles, and Firsts of Our American Presidents.* Layton, Utah: Gibbs Smith, 2007.

Maraniss, David. "Though Obama Had to Leave to Find Himself, It Is Hawaii that Made His Rise Possible." WashingtonPost.com, Friday, August 22, 2008.

McCullough, David. *Truman.* New York: Simon & Schuster, 1992.

———. *John Adams.* New York: Simon & Schuster, 2001.

Obama, Barack. *Dreams from My Father: A Story of Race and Inheritance.* New York: Times Books, 1995.

Richardson, Albert Deane. *A Personal History of Ulysses S. Grant.* Hartford, Conneticut: American Publishing Co., 1868. Google Books e-book.

Scott, Janny. *A Singular Woman: The Untold Story of Barack Obama's Mother.* New York: Riverhead Books, 2011.

Wead, Doug. *The Raising of a President: The Mothers and Fathers of Our Nation's Leaders.* New York: Atria Books, 2005.

Withey, Lynne. *Dearest Friend: A Life of Abigail Adams.* New York: Simon & Schuster, 1981.

ACKNOWLEDGMENTS AND AUTHOR'S NOTE

First Mothers began more than six years ago at a lunch with fellow writers. The conversation started with news of our families and current writing and illustration projects. When we moved on to politics and the current president, one writer mused about the president's upbringing and what his mother must be thinking right now. We realized that aside from Abigail Adams, Sarah Delano Roosevelt, and Barbara Bush, we knew nothing about the presidents' mothers. There are thousands of books about the presidents, hundreds about their wives, and even books about the presidential dog, but only a handful about the women who raised our leaders.

During our three years of research, we discovered that the mothers were as varied as the presidents they raised. Some mothers came from wealthy families, while others brought up their sons in poverty. At least a dozen mothers never learned to read or write, while others were highly educated. There were mothers who doted on their sons and mothers who still offered their motherly advice even when their sons were in the Oval Office. Despite their differences, these forty-three mothers and one stepmother seemed to have several things in common: they all valued learning and made great sacrifices to insure that the future presidents were well educated. They encouraged their sons to pursue their passion and respect hard work.

There is a vast amount of research that goes into a project like this. Aside from the hundreds of books and websites we studied, the National Portrait Gallery was a wonderful resource for portraits of the mothers. The librarians at the San Francisco Public Library found books and magazines about costumes and interiors and were more thorough than any Google search. The museums at Colonial Williamsburg were invaluable for research about colonial life, including that on writing instruments, inkpots, and inkstands, and the costume collection at the Victoria and Albert Museum provided excellent examples of changing fashions.

One book even used *First Mothers* as a title. Since titles are not copyrighted, there are now two books called *First Mothers*. Friends can't wait to challenge us with questions about which mother did what, to see if we know our facts, and usually we do.

This book was lucky to have an overabundance of "mothers" who offered advice and gave suggestions. Our thanks to Susan Meyers, Marilyn Sachs, and Jane Cutler, who were there at the beginning. To Ashley Wolff, Lisa Brown, Christy Hale, and Katherine Tillotson, who lent their expert eyes to the art. And finally, a big thank-you to all the wonderful mothers at Clarion Books, especially Jennifer Wingertzahn, Daniel Nayeri, and Sharismar Rodriguez, who edited, advised, and designed the book.